LUMPS, BUMPS, AND RASHES

LUMPS, BUMPS, AND RASHES

BY ALAN E. NOURSE, M.D.

A First Book/Revised Edition
New York/London/Toronto/Sydney
Franklin Watts/1990

Cover Photographs courtesy of:
Photo Researchers/Biophoto Associates/Lowell Georgia/M. Abbey
Photographs courtesy of: Photo Researchers: pp. 9 (Blair Seitz), 10
(Biophoto Associates/Science Source), 27 (Science Photo Library),
29 (M. Abbey), 33 (Larry Mulvehill), 39 (Lowell Georgia), 43 left
(John Watney), 43 right (Biophoto Associates/Science Source);
Brown Brothers: p. 12; Gamma-Liaison: p. 13 (Forrest Anderson);
Randy Matusow: pp. 14, 21, 25, 36; Monkmeyer Press Photo: p. 17
(Michael Heron); Rothco Cartoons: p. 40 (Engelman); UPI/Bettmann
Newsphotos: p. 49; Jeff Greenberg: p. 51

Library of Congress Cataloging-in-Publication Data

Nourse, Alan Edward.
Lumps, bumps, and rashes : a look at kids' diseases / by Alan E.
Nourse. —Rev. ed., 2nd ed.
p. cm.—(A First book)
Summary: Examines rashes, infections, and other common childhood diseases
and describes methods of curing them or vaccinations to prevent them.
ISBN 0-531-10865-1
1. Communicable diseases in children—Juvenile literature.
[1. Communicable diseases.] I. Title. II. Series.
RJ401.N68   1990
618.92'9—dc20   90-32785   CIP   AC

Contents

1
Who's Sick?

The Brown family have a problem. They are about to leave with their son Johnny, age ten, for a trip to Disney World. But at breakfast Johnny's mother takes one look at him and says, "Uh, oh!" On the middle of his forehead is a small, round water blister that looks exactly like a teardrop. There's another one behind his ear and two more on his chest. In a few hours a dozen more have popped up here and there. Johnny still feels okay, but the vacation trip is postponed.

Is Johnny sick? Yes, indeed. The next morning he is covered head to toe with blisters that are turning red and itching fiercely. His head hurts. He has a temperature of 101° F, and he feels terrible. It will be a week or more before all those blisters crust and peel as Johnny Brown recovers from one of the most contagious of all kids' diseases, **varicella**—better known as *chicken pox*. (A contagious disease is one that can be caught from another person or animal.)

Paul D., age nine, has a problem. He comes home from school one November afternoon coughing and sneezing. His nose is running like a river and his voice is hoarse. He has a slight temperature. But his mother isn't worried—she's seen this kid's disease before.

Is Paul D. sick? Yes, indeed, and he won't feel too good for another three or four days. Paul has caught a common *head cold*. The cold is caused by a **virus** (a very tiny germ) that attacks the nose, throat, and ears. If his cough or fever get worse, his mother will call the doctor. Otherwise, there's not much to do. Doctors say if you take medicine for a cold it will clear up in about seven days, but if you don't do anything it will take a week. That's supposed to be a joke, but Paul doesn't think it's very funny.

Janet M., age thirteen, has a more serious problem. She wakes up one morning with a very sore throat, and feels so cold her teeth are chattering. She can barely swallow her breakfast, and then throws up.

A pediatrician checks the throat of a patient in the course of a routine examination. If the patient's throat is inflamed, the doctor will take a mucus specimen to determine infection.

Her temperature is 104° F. Her mother takes her to see a **pediatrician**—a children's doctor. He examines her throat and ears, and takes a specimen of mucus from her throat for some tests. Then he orders an **antibiotic** (a medicine that kills disease germs).

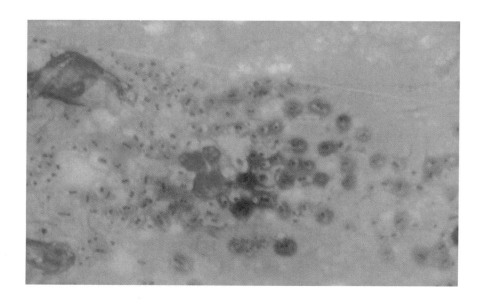

Streptococcus bacteria, the bacteria that causes strep throat, seen through a microscope

Is Janet M. sick? She certainly is, and it isn't just a head cold. Jan has a *strep throat,* a serious throat infection caused by a germ called a **streptococcus.** Two of Jan's classmates came down with the same thing the week before. Because a strep infection can lead to bad trouble later, her doctor wants to kill the germ quickly with medicine before it can spread.

Johnny, Paul, and Janet all had what are often called "children's diseases." These are infections that seem to single out young people in particular. (Of course, adults can get head colds and strep throats, too, but not nearly as often as children do.)

Most children's diseases are caused by germs called **bacteria** or **viruses**. (Bacteria are plantlike cells so small that powerful microscopes are needed to see them. Some bacteria cause infections and some don't. Viruses are even tinier disease-producing particles.)

Some children's diseases, such as chicken pox, are very contagious. They can sweep through whole classrooms or towns in *epidemics*. Almost everyone who is not immune gets sick. Other children's diseases just strike here and there, but sooner or later everybody gets one or another of them. Depending on what part of the body they attack, invading bacteria or viruses may cause a variety of lumps, bumps, or rashes, and make a person feel terrible. Many of them, in fact, produce special "giveaway" symptoms or characteristics that are quite easy to diagnose or identify.

Some of these diseases are harmless. You just wait for your body to drive them away. Some of the diseases are dangerous, but can be treated with antibiotics. Others can be prevented by means of vaccinations or "shots." (For more on vaccinations, see page 46.)

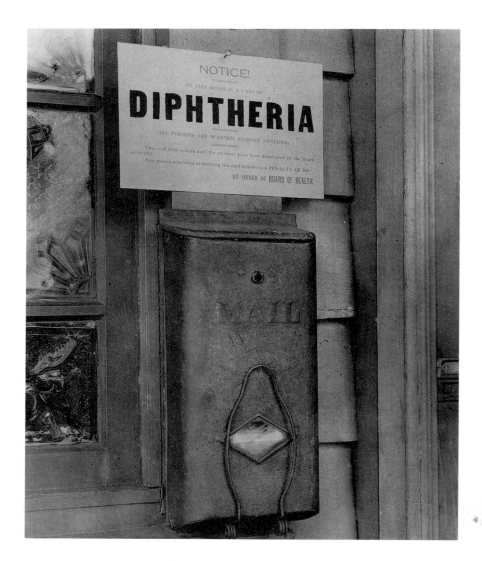

Before certain children's diseases were eliminated by vaccinations, an entire household was placed in quarantine to prevent the spread of the disease.

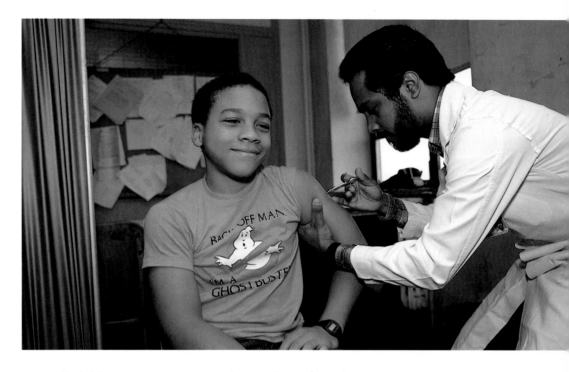

All children are now routinely vaccinated against
diseases that were once considered deadly.

Of course, children can have many diseases that
aren't infections. But infectious diseases are by far
the most common, so we'll look at these in this
book. Mild or severe, these are the diseases everyone should know about. But before we talk about
individual diseases, we need some basic facts about
how infectious diseases generally affect the body.

13

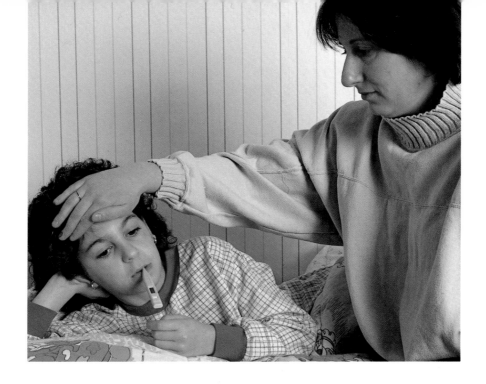

When a fever is present, body temperature has
risen and can actually be felt on the skin.

INFECTION AND
FEVER

Fever is an abnormal rise in body temperature.
It is a sign that an infection has started somewhere.
A number of other things can also cause a fever. But
whenever someone develops a fever, it means
something has gone wrong. And ninety-nine times out
of a hundred, that "something" is an infection.

What brings on a fever? Many chemical reactions in the body's cells produce heat. These reactions work best when the inside body temperature is roughly 98.6° F. Your body has wonderful ways to keep that temperature just about right. But when bacteria or viruses invade the body, your "body thermostat" is thrown out of whack. The body defends itself against these invaders. Many internal chemical reactions speed up, producing heat faster than you can get rid of it, and the temperature rises. Sometimes the invading bacteria manufacture poisons called **pyrogens** (literally, "fire makers") which affect the temperature-control centers and make the fever rise higher. Some viruses do the same thing.

CHILLS, HEADACHES, AND "GENERAL MALAISE"

Certain other symptoms often come with fever. If the fever develops quickly, the person may have a *chill*, shivering and feeling so cold that three blankets don't seem to help. Slower-developing fevers may cause reddening of the face, perspiration, or both. The heart beats faster and breathing speeds up. There may be a headache, joint aches, loss of appetite, even vomiting, along with the fever. In addition, many infections (especially those caused by viruses) cause muscle aches all over the body and a feeling of great tiredness. Doctors call this condition *general malaise* (another way of saying "feeling bad all over"). This is another important clue that some infection is present.

LUMPS, BUMPS, AND RASHES

In some childhood infections, the **lymph nodes** become swollen and tender. Lymph nodes are small lumps of tissue clustered in such places as the armpits and groin, under the lower jaw, or behind the ears. They play an important part in the body's **immune system**—our natural, built-in defense system against infections. Lymph nodes are normally so small and soft you can't feel them at all. But in certain infections they become large, lumpy, and sore.

Infections can produce other telltale swellings too. In *rubeola* (measles), the area around the eyes may become swollen and puffy. In throat infections, the tonsils—two soft oval lumps at the back of the throat—often become swollen. In *mumps,* the glands in the cheeks and under the chin that produce saliva become swollen and sore, so that the person's cheeks look "bumpy."

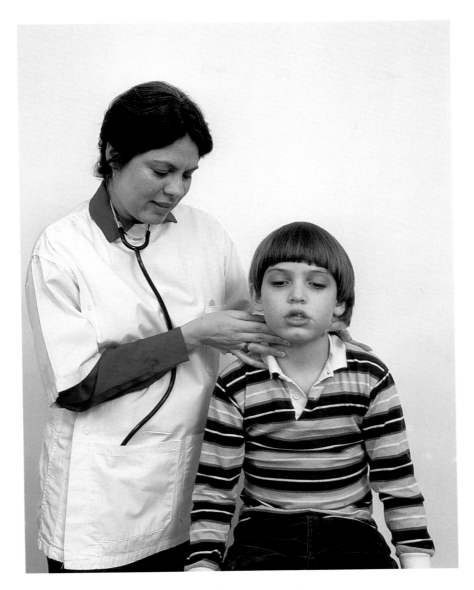

When lymph nodes are infected, a pediatrician can feel them because they become large and lumpy.

Finally, some childhood infections are accompanied by skin rashes. These may range from the fine, bright red flush of some strep infections to the brownish red spots of measles or the teardrop blisters of chicken pox. Such rashes can help a doctor identify the infection.

In this book we'll talk about some of the kids' diseases you're most likely to hear about. Some are just nuisances, but some can be serious. And some are diseases that kids used to get but usually don't get any more because they are protected by shots or *vaccines*. We'll start with a group of infections practically *everybody* gets: the *upper respiratory infections,* or URIs.

2
Upper Respiratory Infections (URIs)

It doesn't matter who you are, you're going to have an *upper respiratory infection,* or URI, every now and then, and there's nothing you can do about it.

One of the easiest ways for disease germs to get into your body from the outside is through your nose and mouth. You're breathing in air all the time, and that air is filled with bacteria and viruses. The pink membrane that lines your nose and throat and bronchial tubes leading to your lungs (the area a doctor calls the "upper respiratory tract") is always moist and warm—a perfect place for germs to lodge and grow. This is why URIs are the most common of all kids' infections.

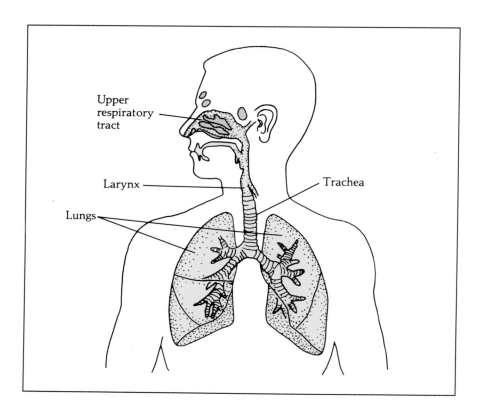

An upper respiratory infection can affect almost any part of
the respiratory system. Sneezing, a runny nose, and a cough
are all signals that this type of infection is present.

HEAD COLDS

These are the most common of all infections.
You don't get colds from getting chilled or sitting in
a draft. Many of them are caused by viruses known
as *rhinoviruses* ("rhino", as in rhinoceros, is a Greek

word meaning "nose"). The viruses invade the cells lining your nose and throat and begin multiplying, causing itching, sneezing, and coughing. Your eyes water, your nose starts running, your throat feels raw, and you may have a temperature of up to 100° or 101° F (compared to a normal temperature of about 98.6° F). Other viruses called *adenoviruses* can cause similar symptoms.

A digital thermometer accurately registers a rise in temperature.

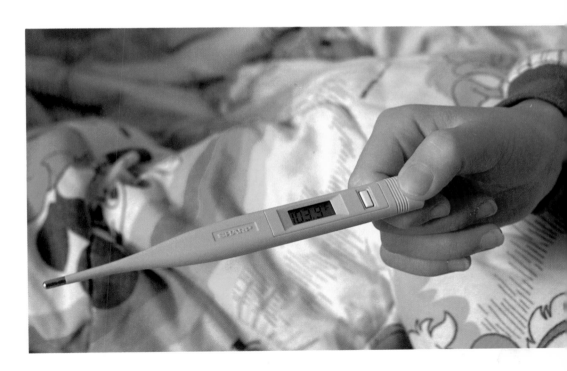

There are no medicines to kill these viruses, so you just have to wait for your body's natural *immune system* to fight them off. This takes about a week or so. Meanwhile, just resting and drinking lots of fluids will help. Nose drops or a nasal spray will help dry up your nose, and an antifever medicine such as aspirin or Tylenol℠ will make you feel more comfortable.

Sometimes a head cold can become *complicated* when bacteria as well as viruses set up housekeeping in the injured cells. Then your nose may plug up with thick, sticky stuff and your throat gets sorer and sorer. If this happens, your doctor may decide to order an *antibiotic* medicine to kill the bacteria and speed your recovery.

SORE THROAT OR
TONSILLITIS

Two different kinds of bacteria frequently invade cells in the throat or the *tonsils*—little oval lumps of tissue in the back of your throat. One is called *staphylococcus* or "staph." The other is *streptococcus* or "strep." Either one can cause a sore, swollen throat and a fever. A *strep throat* is the worst, because the strep germs make a poison that can make you feel sick all over. Your throat becomes very red, and you can often see little yellow

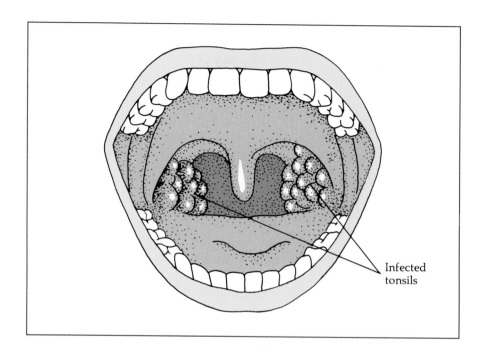

Infected
tonsils

When tonsils become swollen and inflamed,
tonsillitis is probably the cause.

patches of pus on your tonsils. Sore throats can be more serious than head colds, and your doctor may prescribe an antibiotic to kill the bacteria as soon as he or she knows what's happening.

With sore throats, the tonsils are often the main target for infection. In the past, when a child had frequent bouts of tonsillitis, the doctor would take the tonsils out, along with similar patches of infected tissue in the back of the nose, called the *adenoids.* This operation was called *tonsillectomy and adenoidectomy,* or T&A for short. Today most doctors believe this operation won't really help, and actually may do harm in some cases. The tonsils and adenoids trap bacteria before they can travel down into the lungs to cause a more serious infection, *pneumonia.* Also they may help the body build up natural *immunity* to later URIs. So T&As are not performed nearly as often now as they used to be.

MIDDLE EAR INFECTIONS

One common complication of nose or throat infections is the spread of the infection to the middle ear, causing *otitis media,* or earache. The bacteria or viruses find their way up into your ear through a tube that connects your throat with your middle ear. (Your ears "pop" when air passes through that tube.) Earaches of this sort can be very painful, and antibiotics are usually ordered to help control these infections.

CROUP

Just below your throat is your voice box or *larynx.* When bacteria or viruses attack this area, your voice becomes hoarse and squeaky, and sounds

When viruses or bacteria cause throat irritation,
a steamer or humidifier makes breathing easier.

odd. You may even lose your voice, temporarily.
When you cough because of the irritation, your
cough becomes loud or *croupy*, like a seal's bark,
and it *hurts* to cough. It helps to use a *steamer* near
the bed to provide very moist air to breathe. For
older children, croup is mostly just a bother, but for

a baby it can be dangerous. Swelling inside the baby's tiny larynx can actually cut off air to the lungs. So when a baby gets a croupy cough, the doctor should be called right away.

BRONCHITIS

The *trachea* is the big air tube carrying air down from your throat into your chest. It forks into two *main bronchi,* one to either lung. Those main air tubes then branch into smaller and smaller bronchi. When bacteria or viruses invade the cells lining the trachea or bronchial tubes, the infection is called *bronchitis.* The main symptom is coughing and coughing and *coughing.* One time, Mike T. had a spell of coughing from bronchitis in a movie theater that annoyed everyone else and the manager asked him to leave! The coughing may be dry at first, but soon you begin coughing up sticky stuff called *sputum.* Bronchitis is usually accompanied by fever, and you may have trouble sleeping because of the coughing.

This kind of infection is almost always treated with antibiotics. Even if it starts with a virus, bacteria usually come along to make it worse. Sometimes a cough syrup may "loosen up" the cough and help relieve the irritation so you don't cough so

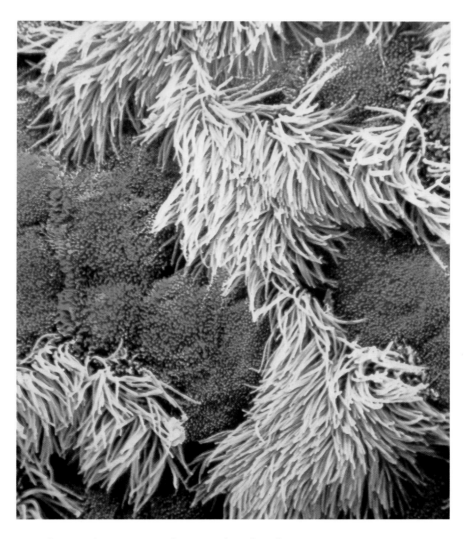

The trachea, or windpipe, is lined with yellowish, grasslike projections called *cilia.* These cilia sweep the trachea and act as a filter for incoming air.

27

much. With treatment, bronchitis will usually clear up in a week or so, but sometimes it lingers for weeks before it's completely healed.

PNEUMONIA

Strictly speaking, this isn't an *upper* respiratory infection, because pneumonia is an infection of the *lower* respiratory tract or lungs. In some cases the lungs are the first target of infection by bacteria or viruses. Other times pneumonia develops as a complication of an earlier URI. It can also occur as a complication of a more widespread virus infection, called *influenza* or "flu." The most common bacteria involved in pneumonia are the *pneumococci*. Fortunately, these germs can be quickly killed by many different antibiotics. But *any* pneumonia can make you very sick, with a high fever, coughing, pain in the chest, and difficult breathing. Recovery may take two to three weeks or more.

INFLUENZA
OR "FLU"

This isn't solely an upper respiratory infection either. The virus that causes it produces a body-wide infection, but prominent in upper respiratory

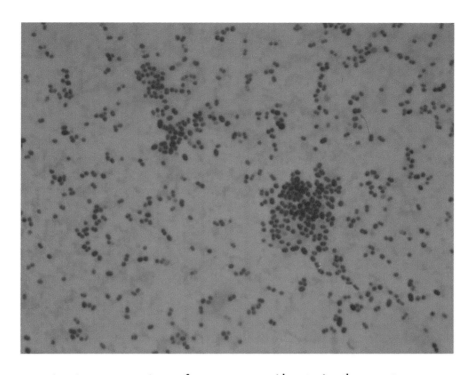

A microscope view of *pneumococci* bacteria, the most common bacteria that causes pneumonia

symptoms are fever, headache, coughing, and sore throat. This infection is also marked by aching muscles and extreme fatigue. There is no treatment for flu except rest, plenty of fluids, an antifever medicine, and lots of patience. It usually clears up in one to two weeks. ***Special warning:*** Children or teenagers suspected of having either flu or chicken pox

should not be given aspirin in any form. A dangerous complication called **Reye Syndrome,** including swelling of the brain, may result. *Ask your doctor to recommend a safe antifever medicine.*

URIs occur much more often in children than in adults. But over the years your body *does* gradually build up immunity to many of the viruses and bacteria that cause URIs, so you don't get them so often. In a sense, you just outgrow them!

3
Children's
Rash Diseases

Some of the most familiar children's diseases are accompanied by skin rashes of one sort or another. Most (but not all) are caused by viruses. Some of these infections can now be prevented by "shots" or vaccinations during childhood, but some cannot. (For more about children's "shots" see Chapter 4.)

VARICELLA
(CHICKEN POX)

You may never have heard of *varicella* before, but you certainly have heard of chicken pox. This common infection is so contagious that about 98 out of every 100 children in the United States get it between the ages of one and ten. It's caused by a

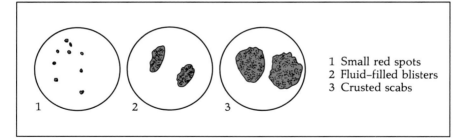

1 Small red spots
2 Fluid–filled blisters
3 Crusted scabs

There are three stages in the development of
chicken pox. In the first, small red spots
appear. Then the spots enlarge and fill with
fluid, raising blisters. In the last stage,
the blisters burst, dry out, and crust over.

virus that spreads easily from person to person in
the droplets sprayed from the nose or throat of an
infected person.

About fourteen days after exposure, the infected
person develops a headache, a low fever, and a little
achiness. Then, within twenty-four hours, the un-
mistakable chicken pox rash appears—small, clear,
teardrop blisters on the skin called *vesicles*. After a
few hours, red rings appear around the blisters,
and they begin to itch fiercely. Over the next few
days, three or four "crops" of new blisters appear,
about a day apart, all over the body—on the face,
neck, palms, feet, even inside the cheeks! New blisters appear while the old ones are drying up. The

fever and achiness are the worst about a day after the rash appears. Then the patient begins feeling better, except that he or she *looks* horrid and itches all over.

There isn't much to do for chicken pox but wait for it to go away. *Don't scratch the blisters*—this could get them infected with strep or staph germs, which could cause scars when they heal. Keep your fingernails clipped as short as possible. A bath in

A case of chicken pox once blisters have appeared

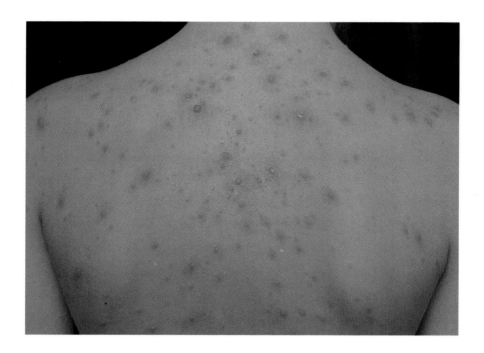

warm soapy water, and calamine lotion on the blisters, will help control the itching. Gradually the blisters fill with pus. Then they crust and dry up, and heal without scars if they haven't gotten infected.

Recently, a vaccine to prevent chicken pox has been tested in Japan and other countries. It has not yet been approved for use in the United States. Prevention could protect children with weak immune systems from bad complications of chicken pox. It could also ensure that young mothers don't infect their unborn babies when they are pregnant. But many doctors think it may be best for normal, healthy children to just "pay their dues"—catch chicken pox, and get it over with.

THE MEASLES DISEASES

Many people think that measles are just measles. Actually, measles is just one of a whole family of virus infections that produce high fevers, red skin rashes, and other irritating symptoms. Some of these infections are harmless, but others can cause real problems.

Rubeola (measles, red measles, hard measles, etc.) is the best known of these diseases. The virus spreads in water droplets which infected people spray when they cough, sneeze, or even just speak. Measles is *very* contagious. Believe it or not, if you put one hundred kids who had never had measles or measles shots in a room for twenty minutes with one kid who has measles, some two weeks later about ninety-seven of the hundred kids would have measles—that's how contagious it is! Symptoms begin seven to fourteen days after exposure, with a sudden high fever, a runny nose, sore, itchy eyes, a sore throat, and a hacky cough. Little white specks called *Koplik's spots* appear inside the cheeks, a "giveaway" sign of measles. Then a reddish-brown, spotty rash appears all over the body, sometimes so thick the spots run together into blotches.

There's no treatment for measles except to stay in bed, drink lots of fluids (to help with the fever), and wait. Calamine lotion helps ease the itchy rash. Most measles patients begin to feel better in a week or so, as the rash starts to fade. But some aren't so fortunate. Occasionally the virus may attack the brain, causing *encephalitis* (brain fever), which can lead to permanent brain damage. And some people have complicating bacterial infections such as *pneumonia* (an infection of lung tissue) or *otitis media* (middle ear infection). Because of these threats, sci-

About the only thing you can do for measles, if you get them, is to wait it out. Spreading calamine lotion on the skin helps to ease the itchy rash.

entists developed a *rubeola vaccine* in 1960, hoping that measles shots given to all babies would quickly wipe out measles. For a while measles all over the country dropped to a few hundred cases a year. But recently, large outbreaks have been occurring in

36

spite of vaccination programs. Doctors are now rec-ommending *booster shots* of the measles vaccine for older children.

Rubella, sometimes called **German measles, light measles,** or **three-day measles,** is a much milder measles-like virus disease. It, too, is spread by droplet infection. Symptoms begin two or three weeks after exposure. They include a fever, a runny nose, and a feeling of tiredness or malaise. A fine red rash appears all over the body for about three days, and then fades away. Most patients feel com-pletely well by the time the rash is gone. Compli-cations seldom occur and, like measles, one attack makes you immune for life.

For years, rubella seemed more a nuisance than a real illness. But in the 1940s it was found that many babies of mothers who had rubella early in their pregnancies were born with serious physical defects—badly formed hearts, blindness, or deaf-ness, for example. The virus didn't hurt the mother, but it was devastating to the developing baby. By 1968 a *rubella vaccine* was developed. Today rubella and rubeola vaccines are often combined in a single shot, together with a vaccine for *mumps,* and rec-ommended for all children. And girls approaching the age of ten or eleven who are not sure they've had rubella, or if they've had a shot against it, should be vaccinated without delay to protect against the risk of someday bearing a rubella-deformed baby.

Roseola infantum is a measles-like disease you may never have heard of. That's not surprising, because it usually occurs in children under the age of two, and often isn't even diagnosed. The baby suddenly runs a very high fever (up to 105° F) for two or three days and then develops a fine red rash like paprika sprinkled all over the body. The rash appears for only a few hours—it can come and go during the night and never even be noticed—and then the disease is over. There is no treatment other than sponge baths to keep the fever down, and no serious aftereffects. Roseola infantum is named for the rosy rash and the usual age of the victim. Sometimes it is called **"fourth disease"** to set it apart from the three more familiar red-rash diseases— rubeola, rubella, and scarlet fever. (For more about scarlet fever, see p. 41.) Like other measles infections, one attack of roseola produces a lifelong immunity.

You may know someone who claims to have had measles or German measles more than once. This isn't likely because of the immunity these diseases confer. Probably that person has actually been infected with some other mild measles-like virus

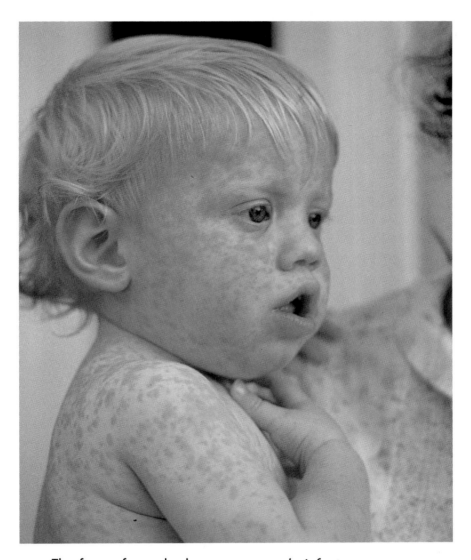

The form of measles known as *roseola infantum*
usually only strikes children under the age of two.
This infant now has lifelong immunity to it.

"It's a thank you card from Jimmy for
giving him the measles."

that just hasn't been identified yet. These offbeat
infections are sometimes called **"fifth disease"** just
to give them a name. They can cause fever, cough,
runny noses, and even red skin rashes. They aren't
serious or long-lasting, and have no known complications.

SCARLET FEVER
(SCARLATINA)

Until the early 1940s, another red-rash disease called **scarlet fever** or **scarlatina** was almost as common as measles, and a good deal more dangerous because of its possible aftereffects. Basically, it is a strep-throat infection caused by a particularly bad strain of streptococcus bacteria. The early symptoms are fever, a very painful sore throat, headache, and vomiting. Often victims feel so weak they can hardly get out of bed to go to the bathroom.

Within twenty-four hours, the patient's throat is covered by a gray coating largely made up of dead cells. The insides of the cheeks are red, the tongue red and sore. Then a fine, red rash appears, first on the neck and inside the arms, then spreading to the rest of the body. Often the rash turns the creases of the neck and the inside of elbows bright scarlet.

The rash is caused by a special *toxin* or poison this strep germ manufactures. Before antibiotics, it took the body three to four weeks to throw off the infection. Many patients, especially babies, died during the severe, early stages of the illness. Others got middle-ear infections, or pneumonia, or even blood poisoning when the strep germs spread into the bloodstream. And damage could occur later to the kidneys or to the heart muscle and valves, because of reactions to the strep toxin.

Fortunately, this particular strep germ was quickly killed by *sulfa drugs* or *penicillin* when they were first used in the 1940s. Today full-blown cases of scarlet fever are seldom seen because doctors treat strep throats with antibiotics very early, before the germs can really take hold. You'll recall that when Janet M. (Chapter One) came down with a strep throat, her doctor ordered an antibiotic right away to prevent any bad effects from the infection.

SKIN INFECTIONS

Some common skin infections occur most often in kids. **Impetigo** is almost always caused by staph or strep bacteria that have gotten through the outer layer of skin and infected the cells underneath. The infection starts with small, raised, itchy blisters. In a few hours the blisters break and form gray, crusty scabs which also itch. Scratching doesn't help. It just spreads the infection. Antibiotic salves or creams will usually stop the itching in a few hours, and get rid of the infection in a day or two. Impetigo is sometimes very contagious, so if you get it, others in your family or classroom may, too.

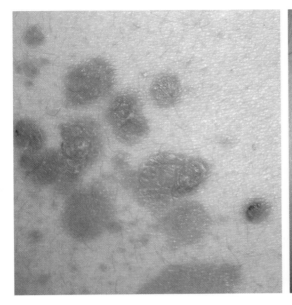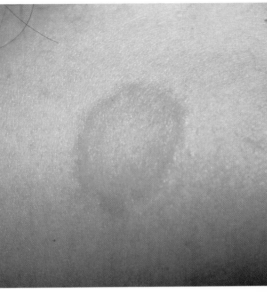

Left: Impetigo blisters that have broken and
crusted over.
Right: The telltale shape and color
of this skin fungus signals that it is ringworm.

Ringworm has nothing to do with a worm—it's
caused by a germ called a *fungus* that infects the
skin and sometimes looks like impetigo. It usually
occurs on the body or in the scalp. The round, itchy
patches get larger by spreading at the edges. (Similar funguses cause "athlete's foot" between the
toes, or "jock itch" in the groin.) Most cases of ring-

worm clear up with the help of an antifungus ointment, but healing may take several weeks.

Acute conjunctivitis or **"pinkeye"** isn't exactly a skin infection, but it is caused by the same kinds of bacteria that cause impetigo, and it sometimes spreads like wildfire in a classroom. The germs attack the delicate, moist inner lining of the eye. The eye becomes suddenly red and itchy, and then begins to ache. The eyelid may get puffy, and a thick discharge forms in the eye. Needless to say, *any* irritation of the eye should be called to a doctor's attention without delay. This infection can be quickly cured by antibiotic drops or salves made specially for use in the eye.

4
Preventable Infections

Some of the most dangerous of all the infectious diseases hardly ever occur anymore in modern countries, because people have been protected against them from early childhood by "shots" or *vaccinations.*

Look at your friends around you. How many have ever had whooping cough? Very few, if any. What about diphtheria? In 1987 there were only three cases reported in the entire country. Yet there was a time when practically *all* children had whooping cough, and diphtheria swept the country in deadly waves. In the 1930s and 1940s, paralytic poliomyelitis ("polio"), one of the most frightening diseases known, crippled or killed as many as 50,000 Americans a year. But in 1987 *not one single case* was recorded in the United States, according to the U.S. Public Health Service. And all because of vaccinations.

Not all of these deadly infections were only *children's* diseases. But all of them struck children as well as others, and the shots to protect against them are best given during early childhood.

ABOUT VACCINATIONS

We've already mentioned that such diseases as chicken pox, measles, or German measles generally occur only once in each person. The body fights them off, and thus becomes *immune* to the germs that cause them. This means that if the same germs return sometime later, they can't cause that same infection all over again. Usually this immunity lasts a lifetime.

It is the body's natural, built-in defense system, called *the immune system,* that fights down these infections when they occur, and then "remembers" the germs and prevents them from causing another infection if they ever return. Scientists have learned that the immune system can recognize just a *part* of an infectious germ—a protein manufactured by the germ that causes tetanus or "lockjaw," for example, or a part of the protein envelope that surrounds

46

a virus particle. Then the immune system can form an immune reaction against the harmless part just as if it were the whole dangerous germ. If a harmless part of a germ is made into a serum and injected into a person before any infection has occurred—in early childhood, for example—the immune system reacts exactly as if the whole germ had come along, and sets up a wall of immunity against the infection. Then, when the whole germ *does* come along later, it can't get a foothold in the body at all. The person is *protected in advance*. (Sometimes the serum or *vaccine* contains just a part of the germ. But in other cases it may contain the whole germ that has been killed or badly weakened, so that it can't itself cause infection.)

BAD DISEASES
YOU NEVER HAVE
TO HAVE

Vaccinations, or "shots," now prevent some of the deadliest of all infections from ever occurring. **Pertussis** or **"whooping cough,"** for example, is a bad, very contagious lung infection that strikes unprotected children of all ages, but mostly children under age two. It causes a sticky, irritating mucus to plug up the air tubes, accounting for the "giveaway" symptom: long bouts of coughing followed by a deep "whooping" intake of breath. Many children used to die from whooping cough. Others ended up with permanently damaged lungs. Children today receive their first shots against whooping cough as early as two months of age, followed by a series of *follow-up* or *booster* shots. Even with widespread vaccination there were still over 2,800 cases of whooping cough reported in the United States in 1987, so it isn't truly a "dead disease."

The whooping cough shot today is given combined with two other vaccines, one against **tetanus,** or "lockjaw," and one against **diphtheria,** in the DTP (*d*iphtheria/*t*etanus/*p*ertussis) shots. Diphtheria is a terrible throat infection that can lead to suffocation. The germ that causes it also makes a powerful poison or *toxin* that can permanently damage the heart, kidneys, or nervous system. Tetanus germs are picked up from the ground in deep cuts and puncture wounds. These germs produce another kind of deadly poison that attacks the nerves and causes clenching of muscles all over the body.

Poliomyelitis ("polio" or "infantile paralysis") was a terrible scourge during the 1930s and 1940s. It was caused by a virus that attacked nerve cells in the brain and spinal cord. There was no way to

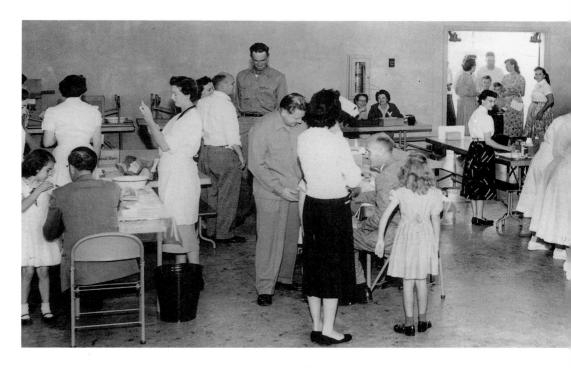

In the first mass vaccination of schoolchildren in
1955, doctors administer the Salk anti-polio vaccine.

prevent it or cure it. Then, in 1954, Dr. Jonas A.
Salk, of the University of Pittsburgh, perfected a
polio vaccine which was given to 1,800,000 school
children in 1955. Later, Dr. Albert Sabin, of the University of Cincinnati School of Medicine, developed
an improved polio vaccine that could be taken by

mouth and produce longer-lasting protection. To-day children from age two months on up receive the polio vaccine, and the terrible summer polio epidemics are a thing of the past.

Mumps and **hemophilus influenzae meningitis** are two other serious diseases that are now routinely prevented by "baby shots." Mumps is a virus infection of the *salivary glands* located in the cheeks and under the tongue. The infection causes pain and swelling in those glands, along with a high fever for several days. Most cases of mumps clear up in a couple of weeks without any lasting problems. But in older children the virus sometimes also attacks the sex glands—a boy's testicles or a girl's ovaries—and may cause permanent sterility (inability to have children later). Because of this, childhood immunization against mumps is recommended.

Hemophilus influenzae meningitis has nothing whatever to do with "flu." It is an infection of the delicate membrane that lines the brain and spinal cord, caused by bacteria from the *hemophilus* family. It often strikes infants and preschoolers, especially in preschool classes or day care centers. It is dangerous because it often causes permanent damage to the brain, even when it's treated with antibiotics.

A vaccine developed in the early 1980s prevents it, but usually isn't given until a baby is eighteen months old. Scientists are now trying to improve the vaccine so it can be given much earlier, when many cases of the infection occur.

Because the infection *hemophilus influenza meningitis* is so contagious, it can be spread through an entire day-care center.

5
Your Basic
Immunizations

As far as your health is concerned, life is far safer today than it was fifty years ago, thanks to the widespread use of preventive vaccines. Diseases like whooping cough, diphtheria, or polio, which once killed thousands, are rarely seen anymore. This is true even though many children never get their basic "baby shots" at all or the *complete* series of shots and boosters recommended by the U.S. Public Health Service. What might happen if *everybody* did?

Well, let's consider what happened with one deadly infection—a terrible virus disease called **smallpox.** Smallpox used to kill thousands of people every year the world around, and left many more with unsightly pockmark scars on their faces.

Protection against smallpox first began way back in 1796, when an English country physician, Edward Jenner, first proved that a vaccine could prevent the disease. During the 1800s and early 1900s, children and travelers all over the world received smallpox vaccinations. The number of smallpox cases each year dwindled and dwindled. Then, in 1974, thanks to vaccination, the *very last case* of smallpox anywhere in the world was reported, and there hasn't been a single case since. Smallpox was permanently eradicated. Today the only smallpox virus existing on earth is stored in a few carefully guarded laboratories, where it is kept for necessary scientific research.

And someday this could be the result for measles, polio, or even the virus that causes AIDS.

Vaccinations *work.* But they have to be given at the right times, on the right schedules, to everyone who isn't immune. Doctors had hoped to wipe out measles within a few years after the first measles vaccine was used in 1960, but that didn't happen. The first vaccine wasn't completely effective, and many children never got the shots. With today's modern vaccine, the goal can—and someday *will* be—reached.

On page 54 is a schedule of the **basic immunizations** that are recommended for every child by

BASIC IMMUNIZATIONS*

Age	Vaccination	Remarks
2 months	Diphtheria/Tetanus/Pertussis (DTP) #1	By injection
	Oral Polio Vaccine (OPV) #1	By mouth
4 months	DTP #2	By injection
	OPV #2	By mouth
6 months	DTP #3	By injection
	OPV #3 (in areas of high exposure risk)	By mouth
15 months	OPV #3 (if not given earlier) *completes basic series*	By mouth
	DTP #4 *completes basic series*	By injection
	Measles/Mumps/Rubella Vaccine (MMR)	By injection
18 months	Hemophilus b polysaccharide vaccine (HbCV or HbPV)	By injection
4–6 years	DTP #5 (booster)	By injection
	OPV #4 (booster) both at or before school entry	By mouth
14–16 years	Tetanus/Diphtheria (TD) Repeat every 10 years through life.	By injection

*Adapted from Centers For Disease Control: *Morbidity and Mortality Weekly Report*, April 7, 1989, vol. 38, no. 13.

the United States Public Health Service in 1989, together with the ideal timing for those shots.

First, there are the "triple vaccine" or basic DTP baby shots. These protect against diphtheria, tetanus, and pertussis (whooping cough). Three DTP shots are given about two months apart, and a fourth at fifteen months, with a booster just before entering school.

The second set of immunizations are against polio. The Sabin Oral Polio Vaccine (OPV) is used to protect against all three major strains of polio. You should have had three doses of OPV by mouth at approximately two, four, and six months of age, with a booster at school age.

Then at fifteen months the combined measles/mumps/rubella vaccine (MMR) is given, and at eighteen months the hemophilus influenzae meningitis shot (HbCV). Finally, at age fourteen to sixteen years, a person should have a booster of the tetanus/diphtheria (TD) portion of the DTP vaccine (a pertussis booster isn't necessary), and this should be repeated about every ten years throughout life.

This schedule of basic immunization shots is the best arrangement possible. But most of these shots can safely be given at any age, if the ideal series of shots has been interrupted for some reason, or never started in childhood.

Thanks to modern immunizations, you and your friends can escape the misery and dangers of a number of childhood infectious diseases. It does take time and attention to obtain the basic immunizations and keep them up to date. But preventive immunizations are a wonderful boon to health that everyone, young or old, should take advantage of.

Glossary

Antibiotic: A medicine, like penicillin, that can kill certain bacteria and stop infection.

Bacteria: Tiny, plantlike cells, often called "germs," which sometimes cause infections. Bacteria are too small to be seen with the naked eye, and can be observed only through a microscope.

Body tissue: Any group of cells in the body forming an identifiable structure or organ. Bone is one form of body tissue. Liver cells form another kind. Connective tissue holds bone, skin, and other structures together.

Cell: The basic building block of living matter in all animals and plants.

Chill: An attack of shivering, with a feeling of coldness, which can occur with fever.

Complication: Anything that makes an illness unexpectedly worse than it usually is. A middle ear infection that starts while a person is weakened by measles is an example of a complication.

Contagious: "Catching." A contagious disease is one that can be caught from another person or animal.

Diagnosis: The identification of a particular kind of disease or infection. Sometimes the signs and symptoms alone provide the diagnosis. Sometimes X rays and lab tests also help.

Disease: A sickness or illness; anything that disturbs normal good health.

Epidemic: An outbreak of a contagious disease among many people at the same time.

Fahrenheit: A temperature scale on which the boiling point for water is 212 degrees Fahrenheit. The freezing point for water is 32 degrees Fahrenheit.

Fever: A rise in body temperature above the normal level of 98.6 degrees F. Sometimes just called a "temperature."

Fungus: A plant growth, different from bacteria, that can cause such infections as ringworm and athlete's foot.

General malaise: A condition of muscle aching, tiredness, and just feeling sick that often accompanies infection.

Groin: The area between the legs where the legs join the body.

Immune: Protected or "safe" from catching an infection—either by having had that infection, or by being vaccinated against it.

Immunity: The state of being immune or protected against a certain infection.

Infection: A kind of sickness or illness that can occur when certain bacteria or viruses enter the body.

Lymph nodes: Small lumps of glandlike tissue found in the armpits, the groin, under the angles of the jaw, behind the ears, and in other widely scattered locations. These nodes manufacture lymphocytes and play an important part in the body's defense against infection.

Lymphocytes: A kind of white blood cell manufactured in the lymph nodes and passed into the bloodstream to help fight infection.

Microscope: An instrument far more powerful than a magnifying glass, used by scientists to observe and study bacteria.

Mumps: A contagious or "catching" virus infection of the salivary glands (the saliva-producing organs located in the cheeks and under the chin).

Ovaries: The female sex glands.

Perspiration: The moisture or "sweat" that appears on the skin when we feel too warm.

Protein: One of the basic chemicals that make up cells.

Pyrogens: Poisonous chemicals, manufactured by some bacteria, which can cause fever by affecting the body's temperature-control centers.

Rubella: The medical name for German measles, also known as light measles or three-day measles.

Rubeola: The medical name for measles, also known as common measles, ordinary measles, red measles, hard measles, ten-day measles, or black measles.

Susceptible: Unprotected (that is, without immunity) against a given infection, and therefore likely to catch it if exposed to it.

Symptom: Any change from normal in the body that warns us that something is not quite as it should be. Typical signs or symptoms of infection might include fever, headache, pain, sore throat, coughing, and so forth.

Testicles: The male sex glands.

Tonsils: Two soft oval lumps of body tissue visible at the back of the throat (if they haven't been taken out surgically).

Toxins: Poisonous chemical substances manufactured by certain bacteria and released into the body during infection.

Vaccination: The process of injecting a vaccine into a patient to produce immunity to a given infection.

Vaccine: A medical preparation, often containing material from weakened or destroyed bacteria or viruses. A vaccine can be injected into the body to produce protection or immunity to a given infection.

Varicella: The medical name for chicken pox.

Viruses: Extremely tiny particles, far smaller than bacteria, that often cause infection. Viruses can only be observed with the aid of special electron microscopes.

White blood cells: Special cells in the bloodstream that travel to areas of infection and help destroy invading bacteria.

For Further Reading

Donahue, Parnell, and Helen Capellaro. *Germs Make Me Sick: A Health Handbook for Kids.* New York: Alfred A. Knopf, 1975

Lerner, Marguerite R. *Dear Little Mumps Child.* Minneapolis, Minn.: Lerner Publications, 1959.

Lerner, Marguerite R. *Peter Gets the Chickenpox.* Minneapolis, Minn.: Lerner Publications, 1959

Metos, Thomas H. *Communicable Diseases.* New York: Franklin Watts, 1987.

Nourse, Alan E. *Viruses.* New York: Franklin Watts, 1983.

Patent, Dorothy H. *Germs!* New York: Holiday House, 1983.

Richardson, Joy. *What Happens When You Catch a Cold?* Milwaukee, Wisconsin: Stevens Inc., 1986.

Showers, Paul. *No Measles, No Mumps for Me.* New York: Harper Junior Books, 1980.

Index

Fever, 14–15, *14*
"Fifth disease," 40
Flu (influenza), 28–30
"Fourth disease," 38
Fungi, 42–43, *43*

General malaise, 16
German measles (rubella), 37–38, 46, 55

Head colds, 8, 11, 20–22, 23
Hemophilus influenzae meningitis, 50–51, *51*, 55

Immune system, 16, 22, 46–47
Immunizations, 52–56. *See also* Vaccinations
Impetigo, 42, *43*, 44
Infectious diseases, 13–18
Influenza (flu), 28–30

Jenner, Edward, 53
Jock itch, 43

Koplik's spots, 35

Larynx (voice box), 24–26
Lockjaw (tetanus), 48, 55
Lymph nodes, 16, *17*

Measles diseases, 34–40
    roseola infantum, 38, *39*

rubella, 37–38, 46, 55
rubeola, 16, 18, 34–37, *36*, 38, 53, 55
Middle ear infections, 24, 35, 41
MMR (measles/mumps/rubella) vaccine, 55
Mumps, 16, 37, 50, 55

Otitis media (earache), 24, 35, 41

Penicillin, 42
Pertussis (whooping cough), 45, 47–48, 52, 55
Pinkeye (acute conjunctivitis), 44
Pneumococci bacteria, 28, *29*
Pneumonia, 24, 28, *29*, 35, 41
Poliomyelitis (infantile paralysis), 45–46, 48–50, *49*, 52, 53, 55
Pyrogens, 15

Quarantine, *12*

Rash diseases, 18, 31–44
Reye Syndrome, 30
Rhinoviruses, 20–22
Ringworm, 43–44, *43*
Roseola infantum, 38, *39*

Rubella (German measles), 37–38, 46, 55
Rubeola (measles), 16, 18, 34–37, *36*, 38, 53, 55

Sabin, Albert, 49–50
Sabin Oral Polio Vaccine (OPV), 49–50, 55
Salivary glands, 50
Salk, Jonas A., 49
Scarlet fever (scarlatina), 38, 41–42
Skin infections, 42–44
Skin rashes. *See* Rash diseases
Smallpox, 52–53
Sore throat (tonsillitis), 16, 22–24, *23*
Sputum, 26
Staphylococcus bacteria, 22, 33, 42
Strep throat, 8–10, *10*, 11, 18, 22–23, 41
Streptococcus bacteria, 10, *10*, 22, 33, 41–42
Sulfa drugs, 42

Tetanus (lockjaw), 48, 55

Thermometers, digital, *21*
Tonsillectomy and adenoidectomy (T&A), 24
Tonsillitis (sore throat), 16, 22–24, *23*
Tonsils, 16, 22, 23–24, *23*
Trachea (windpipe), 26, *27*
"Triple vaccine" (DTP shot), 48, 55

Upper respiratory infections (URIs), 19–30, *20*

Vaccinations, 11, *13*, 18, 31, 34, 36–38, 45–51, *49*
    basic immunizations and, 52–56
Varicella (chicken pox), 7–8, 11, 18, 29–30, 31–34, *32*, *33*, 46
Vesicles, 32
Viruses, 8
Voice box (larynx), 24–26

Whooping cough (pertussis), 45, 47–48, 52, 55
Windpipe (trachea), 26, *27*